Swallow

Swallow

POEMS

Miranda Field

A MARINER ORIGINAL
Houghton Mifflin Company
Boston • New York
2002

For Tom, and for Willie and Finnian

I owe endless amounts of gratitude to the following people, for help and support, poetic and otherwise: Catherine Barnett, Susan Bruce, Michael Collier, Christina Davis, Timothy Donnelly, Judy Jensen, James Longenbach, Lynn Melnick, Pamela Rosenblum, Tom Thompson, and Rynn Williams. I also thank Janet Silver, Corrina Lesser, and Liz Duvall at Houghton Mifflin. And I thank my family, most especially my mother, Carla Brelos Cantine Field, and father, John Field, whose voices opened my ear to meaning and music to begin with.

Library of Congress Cataloging-in-Publication data is available.

ISBN 0-618-18930-0

Printed in the United States of America

Book design by Robert Overholtzer

DOC 10 9 8 7 6 5 4 3 2 1

The author gratefully acknowledges the editors of the following publications, in which the listed poems originally appeared: *Agni*: "As the Crow Flies, So Will It Fall"; *Antioch Review*: "Bestial," "Subway"; *Boston Review*: "Bright Ardor," "Housefire," "Hortus Conclusus," "Jack's Lake," "Soloist," "Wedding Night"; *Colorado Review*: "Field Hare"; *Fence*: "Childhood's House," "Tumultuous Stillness"; *The Nation*: "Then As September Fields of Wheat & Straw Take Fire"; *Pleiades*: "At Ravenscroft," "Miraculous Image"; *Post Road*: "Birthmark," "Cock Robin."

CONTENTS

Bread Loaf and the Bakeless Prizes

Since 1926 the Bread Loaf Writers' Conference has convened every August in the shadow of Bread Loaf Mountain, in Vermont's Green Mountains, where Middlebury College maintains a summer campus. The conference, founded by Robert Frost and Willa Cather—a generation before creative writing became a popular course of study—brings together established poets and prose writers, editors, and literary agents to work with writers at various stages of their careers. Frost's plan for the conference included a faculty of distinguished writers who would "turn from correcting grammar in red ink to matching experience in black ink, experience of life and experience of art." Bread Loaf has stayed true to Frost's original vision, and its vibrancy and energy have helped make it the most respected of the many summer writers' conferences in the nation.

While part of Bread Loaf's reputation was built on the writers associated with it — W. H. Auden, Sinclair Lewis, Wallace Stegner, Katherine Anne Porter, William Carlos Williams, Ralph Ellison, Nelson Algren, Toni Morrison, Adrienne Rich, May Sarton, Archibald MacLeish, Frank O'Connor, and Richard Wright, among others — it has an equally high reputation for finding and supporting writers of promise at the earliest stages of their careers. Eudora Welty, Carson McCullers, Anne Sexton, May Swenson, Russell Banks, Joan Didion, Miller Williams, Richard Yates, Richard Ford, Julia Alvarez, Carolyn Forché, Linda Pastan, Dave Smith, Tess Gallagher, Ellen Bryant Voigt, Andrea Barrett, and Tim O'Brien are some of the poets, novelists, and short story writers who benefited from the scholarships and fellowships Bread Loaf awards annually.

The importance of Bread Loaf for American writers is typified by Julia Alvarez's recollection of her first conference: "I went to Bread Loaf for the first time in 1969 and fell in love with the community of writers . . . All these people talking about nothing but writing, forcing me to think about writing! I aspired to this great society." My own relationship with Bread Loaf began in 1981 when I attended as a scholar, and was renewed in 1986 when I returned as a fellow. These initial opportunities allowed me to work with William Stafford and

Philip Levine, whose influence helped to shape the way I think of myself as a writer. Later, as an associate faculty member, and since 1995 as director, I have repeatedly witnessed the profound effect the eleven days in August have on those who attend. John Ciardi, a former director of the conference and one of its most eloquent spokesmen, liked to say about the Bread Loaf experience that "no great writer ever became one in isolation. Somewhere and sometime, if only at the beginning, he had to experience the excitement and intellectual ferment of a group something like this."

There are many obstacles to a successful literary career, but none is more difficult to overcome than the publication of a first book. The Katharine Bakeless Nason Literary Publication Prizes were established in 1995 to expand Bread Loaf's commitment to the support of emerging writers. Endowed by the LZ Francis Foundation, whose directors wished to commemorate Middlebury College patron Katharine Bakeless Nason and to encourage emerging writers, the Bakeless Prizes launch the publication career of a poet, fiction writer, and creative nonfiction writer annually. Winning manuscripts are chosen in an open, national competition by a distinguished judge in each genre. The winning books are published in August to coincide with the Bread Loaf Writers' Conference, and the authors are invited to participate as Bakeless Fellows.

Since they first appeared in 1996, the winning Bakeless books have been critical successes. As a result, the Bakeless Prizes are coveted among new writers. The fact that Houghton Mifflin publishes these books is significant, for it joins together one of America's oldest and most distinguished literary presses with an equally distinguished writers' conference. The collaboration speaks to the commitment of both institutions to cultivate emerging literary artists in order to ensure a richer future for American writing.

MICHAEL COLLIER
Director, Bread Loaf Writers' Conference

Foreword

One of the most annoying things about judging literary contests like the Bakeless Prize is the near impossibility of offering credible praise. Given the overload of superlatives on book-jacket-scapes and reader resistance to this overpainted scenery, it is almost impossible to describe in unclichéd terms the virtues of a collection. If the critic or judge wishes to acknowledge a notable new book, she often is reduced to trotting out tired adjectives like *groundbreaking* and *dazzling* (as in "dazzling debut") — or the ever-recurrent *promising*.

One of the most gratifying things about judging literary contests like the Bakeless Prize, however, is simply getting to read, every blue moon or so, a first collection that really is groundbreaking and dazzling. For *Swallow*, these overused adjectives apply. This *is* a startling and riveting read — this *is* a powerful collection (to what cliché shall I turn now?); this *is* an original voice.

Nothing I might say could come close to paraphrasing the poignancy and authority of these lines from Miranda Field's poem "Subway":

> At first the meaning won't come out from hiding:
> a piston-motion, a tongue-flickering, urgent
> but contained. What it does is not come. What it does is
> hold back and beckon, fire off its small explosion
> in your brain: desire to penetrate the bulwark
>
> distance.

The maturity of style is unexpected, the experienced, empirical feel of the "knowingness" of the lyric is jolting — far beyond what the reader is accustomed to encountering in first books. The power here is contained and reiterative — the motif of "Thread of the Screw" reinforces this darkly musing context, held in, reinscribed.

> The spider in the ripe
> grapes slows, the grapes grow
> full.

What full-blown yet disciplined music is this? The "chimes" of *spider* and *ripe* are almost funny (and filled with literary associations) until the seductive, more melancholy echo of "grapes slows" and "grapes grow/full." The passage's acknowledgment of rhyme and meter is underscored by the eerie slowing down of time within the poem as the spider actually slows before our eyes — perhaps dying as the fruit enlarges, inexorably. What drama in three lines!

The effect is — okay — dazzling and unforgettable:

> Rain falls on the gathered crowd, cold, like fire, doors
> in the great clouds opening on sun and a torn, a messy sunset
> pooling in the cracks of everything.

Miranda Field would be called promising if she hadn't already fulfilled promise in these stunning poems. "And once the wonder/sleeping in a thing unborn comes to that glass . . ." — who knows? Here is a beginning that has the feeling of beginning, middle, end — all stages of maturation of expression. Miranda Field shakes off all apparent influence, all guiding sensibilities — she's on her own:

> Climbing the brambles where the cat is snagged who caught the
>   songbird
> instantly the dark came down.

CAROL MUSKE-DUKES

1

Hortus Conclusus

What kind of wilderness
takes bread and milk
from a blue willow saucer?
A wilderness that trains you
to a feverish faith.
You feed it ceaselessly.
You've fallen
under a type of persuasion
a child's book might call a spell:
how invisible the walls are,
closing in.
Now say it's nothing
but another's body — approximate
to your own, but foreign.
The body must accompany you
everywhere you go. Now tell it something:
it doesn't listen. It hasn't the restraint
to live inside that cultivated space
speech makes. Feed it
from your finger,
a waterdrop with salt dissolved.
This provision is intimate, fiduciary.
Language is intent on entering
its hidden garden.
You ask this hunger for a name.
It sends you looking for one
tumbling on the ground, across the night-
grass into bushes.

Soloist

Above the wall, the sky is plaster-white.
A voice climbs the wall. It disguises itself as creeper or vine,
it falls like milk spilt over the edge of a table,
the voice of the mother, climbing, falling, continuous.
It goes on trailed by other sounds, not liquid at first, but
	electrical.
By the voices of small dogs whose howls and quarrels
rise like cinders, but roll over the lip of the wall
and drip down, singed by cold stone.
And the voices of children, not musical like the mother's, not
	sonorous,
no more so than the animals'. But as idolatrous.
The house has a black door set with jeweled glass.
Jewels fall from the door when the door swings open and bangs
	shut.
The missing jewels are buried in the grass,
the holes healed with flimsier translucencies.
How the world appears through the dissolution of the door's
	window
is disordered, warped, under water. Or as a wooded lot
appears to one lost there. The children lean in unison against the
	glass to look.
They know enough to stay. They know enough to know
they need not push the door to let the mother out.
Her singing passes through divided spaces like a mist. It rises
	like vapor in a still, then starts to fall,
though now and then an errant note will lift itself above the wall.
To follow it would be like tying a string to a bird—
not to the acquisitive magpie swooping down to pluck a jewel
	from the mud.
Some urgencies are tenured to the earth, its treasures.
But some forget us. Some go farther.

Then As September Fields of Wheat & Straw Take Fire

What's withheld till wind parts the grasses:
Musk flooding the air, noxious-sweet—eggshell frail,
the tiny bones of the vole, its velvets stiffened,
pouchful of insects and seeds. Cold stones,
no movement in the tinfoil fallen leaves,
silence in the humus, and shadows on the hill grown long,
the death of the sun, the sun in its brief grave
waiting to be born. The cat hurries a carcass off,
but the deer won't run through the grove.
They could be painted deer, they stand stock-still,
as if they wait, as if they want the gun, the sight's
devotion: Such attentiveness is like a hot gold rush
of air from another content. And the jaws of stupefaction
can't release what they close on, the fears that hound
the hunter's child: *who climbs the larcenous ladder to the shelf*
is caught by the foot . . . The deer's children—all spring long
they come so close to the windows they startle
themselves against the glass. They let us watch them
because it warms them, as when my milk won't come
my newborn thrives on my look—undiluted, nourishing.
Body entering all awe, all shock, who'd hobble you,
who'd bleed you of your want? The striding
shadows on the hill grow long, the hunters anxious—
not hunger driving them, not prescience of winter,
but nostalgia—for the fall about to start, that trapdoor in the air:
ardor to elegy. The painter arranges the deer in the wood.
Ripe fruit. Ready. So rich, so wet the palette.
Blood and iodine, desire and its attendant
damage. The hunter's gun is loaded. The heart of the hunter
heavy as the hunted's. And the chambers divided:
I & thou. And the passage narrow.

Subway

At first the meaning won't come out from hiding:
a piston-motion, a tongue-flickering, urgent
but contained. What it does is not come. What it does is
hold back and beckon, fire off its small explosion
in your brain: desire to penetrate the bulwark

distance. He *wants* you to see. He takes the weaponry
of looking, bends it back. The boy miles off, safe.
The boy untouchable — on the far platform,
such a fortress built between you, such a crow's-nest
distance, and the smile you can't see says

so far off you don't exist . . .

But you are here, and his shape pins the air
above the tracks, lit figure in a black space any eye can enter.
Not public, this place he makes, hammering
the locked dark with his fist, in the slip between rush hours.
Private, though you're invited in.

The boy leans forward, propped by nothing,
his prick in his hand lost in the glittering latitudes
of white, identical tiled walls, then seen, then unseen . . .
Small crux of flesh. Forest of rusted girders. Lost context,
buried city nothing enters without a toll.

And tunnels into it and tunnels out open in the shadows: valves
velvet with soot, the thought opening and shutting:
The train is coming / the train will never come . . .
The ending of the boy's tension, crescendo, holds back,
keeps refusing to yield, to you, to him, insists

it will stay, insists it will always be
about to end — nagging ghost of the choked-off, the buried —
the way a child stands still and holds her breath

until her lips darken, carotids blue and knotted in the frail neck.
See me? Watch me die. In the dark

he will not come. In the dark his work
has no reward, the cap tipped down, the—he could be anyone,
one tile, one shout inside the city's wash of sound—
lottery of flotsam on the downtown platform.
On the walls, urgent scrawls: *In a cradle of sand,*

an endless storm blows . . . but words are old, thoughts
oxidize. Exposure to the rush hour burns, the breathed air
burns. There is a war. There always is. And words
go missing from the messages
that line these walls, signs papered over signs . . .

At (place name erased) *twenty-four-hour workdays*
fill an order for five thousand body bags . . .
Signs speak quietly. Signs whisper,
and workers work overtime, work nights, nights . . .
The bones, tendons

in the white wrist pumping, pulling, so much work
to be done to accomplish one small explosion.
The neurons fire, the mind feeds on the spark—meaning: yes—
motion of stitching?—no—engines?—yes—motion of pistons . . .
Beneath the shut-tight lid, beneath the hood

of any machine, obsessive repetition, invisible hands . . .
It's quiet, the dark air, secretive.
Inviting, this dark cave, smelling of piss, hidden,
though he insists you see, and you work hard to see,
and you work secretly. Not to be seen seeing, yes. Anyone

can enter it like this: the private sector of this public darkness.

Crime Scenes

After Luc Sante's *Evidence*

The bedsheets, clean but mended in places, torn from their corners,
    turn about the eye of a storm.
The wind whips up the snow to fireworks or ambient grasses.
The house the wind roars round shuts tight as a very small child's
    grammar of silence when questioned.
The grasses spark when a sudden brief rush of wind scrawls a gust
    across the snow scene's flawlessly withholding surface.
The wind a bridle with a loop capable of being tightened about the
    middle.
The snow a slow lobbing of blunt-handed blows.
The grasses pyrotechnic. Through a window,
two corpses appear to be nesting together, or one man seems to
    suckle the other,
or eat, or kiss the breastbone of. A picture hangs askew above them
    on the pitted wall, a blind alley.

*

A letter waits, illegible, balanced on a water pitcher near the
    woman whose shoes she fastened while alive,
the one now twisted off.
Blood blooms on her crumpled blouse, between the leg-o'-mutton
    sleeves, but the wound is elsewhere,
the wound might be found inside the doubled-over form, if the coil
    the wounded body has become could be unwound.
The beds and chairs and possessions in the room's undoing
    composition bend at the edges, dragged by the wind.
The restless swarm of gestures and expressions, part unraveled,
    freezes in this wind.
The wind has an urgent message inside it. It is a message the
    image suppresses.
It is hard to see. It is hard to see or hear or feel anything in this
    conscripted wind.

Field Hare

After Dürer

A wild thing held in the arms or in the hand acts like a dying thing. It doesn't need to listen, knows without persuasion to be still—not like a belief in ghosts or gods, but like a faith in air. And air escapes it. It breathes as if its lungs had been replaced by gills, and the water shifted from the world. Or if instead of fear its veins were filled with gratitude. A chill gray northern morning swallowing a ship's hold loaded with equatorial parrots. Birds far from home, sick with a sense that flies from them. Birds woken, shaken loose from their systems like pieces of a small clock, minute hands. Or like the joke told me by the shy Hungarian girl who watches my child. There's a vital crack. It flies past my ear. And I feel nothing but the afterbreeze of wings. And she's shot down. When a thing is lifted from the grass, like an egg from the nest, implanted in the minds of strangers (ectopic, cuckoo), why wouldn't it tense itself against invasion? He traps the animal himself. He keeps it tenderly, as a mother stays her hand from harming what she holds. He saves it from the butcher, dresses it in soft and ever softer strokes of stylus and brush. He feeds it something with the odor of singed hair (bent over the candle to see the subject clearer). Now finds a veil for it to wear, the light that filters from a foreign sky, a sauce heated long and slow enough to gather to itself a subtle undertow. The senses drink, the senses nearly drown in the strange stare. And all the ganglia surrender.

Thread of the Screw

Under a naked sun
among bosomy clusters
the spider discovers sweetness

drives the fly, the bee,
fireworm, the black pest
Phyloxera vastatrix
to visit the vine

& with a twine endless
& beginningless
rigs all the trellises
with traps. Rapture is *the act*

of seizing,
carrying off as prey
or plunder, or

being seized,
moved, as in ascent
to heaven . . .

Turn swallows turn: vines,
bubbling juice,
bombinations of the fumbling
bees, flies.

The spider in the ripe
grapes slows, the grapes grow
full. In town, time

intensifies: bottles to be blown,
corks carved, vine-
hooks sharpened, presses set.

Museum of Natural History

Transfixed, exiled—like the girl's dress
discarded in a mountain stream, tumbling,
tangled in the current for weeks, snagged on a twig
caught between rocks. When the stream freezes,
the motion stops. The elk's head held up dead straight,
but not quite. At an inquisitive angle. Assessing,
or feeling the strangest breeze climb through the leaves.
It seems to scintillate—the world's listening ears
cocked—but only mimics motion, the way
the wind outside in moving trees above the buses
imitates an ocean. People file past slowly,
past the sugary snowcapped peaks, Saharan dusks.
They want to occupy these foreign ranges,
so proximate, so approachable, so palpable, the air
of tundra, moraine . . . *Above the coastal ranges, wreaths*
of cumulonimbus clouds gather, touched by the setting sun . . .
TROPIC, DESERT, FOREST. Sleeves, embroideries
of words; gestures torn off, sheathes
still warm, still holding the bodies' shapes.
A bobcat closes on the kill, freeze-framed on hind legs
above blood-splashed snow, snow that ages,
gathers dust. And next door, bent to dip her muzzle in glassy water
at her feet, an African gazelle, nerve endings mercurial,
mouth seemingly moist at the hinges, the soft opening, velvet
        tongue,
the meager water clean, the wind warm, but harm, harm
in everything. *Listen,* whispers the hair-trigger brain—
a stage whisper, a whisper loud as heavy rain—*this fragile house*
cracks easily as ice . . . And the people looking in might drown
inside themselves (ghosts of motion, residue of sense,
handprints mottle the glass, the blowzy smears of mouths),
the faces press in close, as if they've found the crack
through which a broken moment can be seen entire: *touched*
by the setting sun, Susanna's hair undone . . .

who is she

11

Tumultuous Stillness

An hours-long rescue attempt ended early evening. —*Barnet Press*

The sky arrests like one of those phantasmagoric fabrics
cinquecento angels wear: citron and rose with gold in the folds,
pinholes the color of rubies, and tearing, mended in places:

several kinds of weather stitched together. A fever
with a chill in the folds, shadows like stable doors
into near-Antarctic cold where straw smolders,

decaying, fermentation of pure biology—
the air being like this, no wonder clouds above us
stop. The specific needs to far outshine the general.

And couldn't any of these clouds account for the holes?
Great clods cut from the clay, weighing a ton each, risen
past the horizon line, past the wire fence, over the library,

above even the telephone lines: sheer, elegant suspension—
a moment, death-still, in the crowd when one of the pulleys
starts pulling, when the grappling hook surfaces . . .

No wonder the clouds are sculptural, marble, sepulchral.
The world's contusions goad them to mock death. For the sky
reflects the earth. How like a cockfight this weather is!

Rain falls on the gathered crowd, cold, like fire, doors
in the great clouds opening on sun and a torn, a messy sunset
pooling in the cracks of everything. Each hauled-up

block of heavy mud a planet-worth of guesses
levied on it—how much weight the rain adds to the clay,
the probable pocket of air that cossets him, that keeps him

living. Now Certainty, who stops the heart. As if the crows
know, hooded apostles, how they huddle. The buried man
has come upon some understanding now he hordes, now

gorges on. The world yields. The crows lean in,
the crows cry after him: what is this flight that runs us
ragged? But there's no crying forth from life,

no window to lean out from. Still, the mind thinks itself
a bank of windows, sheer glinting invitations. And once the wonder
sleeping in a thing unborn comes to that glass, the anguished

beating of the wings, the flailing, weeping . . .
flood like a shadow trailing the body where it goes.
The shadow has the man's dimensions, his restlessness,

his shape. But the man has not the shadow's fixed
attention; that escape. Where is it I'll go next? Why can I not wait?
A question mark lodged deep among the roots of poplars—

the body, the blood. Among the roots of nettles,
clumped dock leaves, broken bricks,
between the pipes that carry water to and from the town,

quick, inward-starlit chemistries begin. Warm gases form
a cushion for the corpse, a slow, salt hemorrhage
of just-unbottled troubles leaks into the ground.

As if the world had loosed a whisper from its folds, *hush*,
a motherly admonition, when the earth gives,
the crows rush aloft in one mass exhalation and settle

on wires above the building site. Then night comes
down around them, swallows whole the man-
made things, the made things left behind turned dream.

Citronella

The gnats grow furious. Catch wind of us
from where they wait, far in the tall trees. And the swallows
wait in turn for them. Whom we snub, with whom in mind
we rub the rich oil on our skin—perfume calling them,
keeping them away. The world swarms
round the groggy six-week baby turning in my lap,
the long grass tugging at its tethers. He wants to eat, eat all of it—
the evening's distractions, too-strong lemon
currents rising through the trees. In smoke from the grill
meat and fish burn, sweet-corn burns. The corn came oddly late.
Summer rained and rained and the corn grew old in the rows,
and the baby was overripe—timed an early summer child,
but hesitant. I don't blame him. He waited. He grew
too big listening for the flies to murmur to him from the kitchen.
I cleared the clutter from our rooms to make way for him,
my hands grew hotter every noon, but hell can't hold a candle
to the about-to-be-born. He broke me open. The children scream,
they seem in constant collision, but this is how they play:
with accidents and bandages and balms. The midwife held him up,
his huge head hungry on its stem: too big, too old, too slow,
then sudden: a son. Not the girl I wanted. The boy slit me.
And the children kick the lemons littering the ground,
soccer balls—but yellower than sulfur, brighter than the suns
tacked on the kitchen wall: children's suns—alive, leering,
many-tentacled. The late sun licks them, but the lemons won't
        respond.
The tree is only ornamental. The glowing lemons smell of nothing,
but the children kick them till they split, and look how full they
        grow.
Ants crowd in, small birds eat the seeds. The tree is a rare strain—
bred for looking only. But the children open up the lemons
and the small birds eat and grow too full to fly away.

Miraculous Image

When an effigy cries,
        the wood she's carved from rots.
Tears, tight-reined, migrainous
        implosions. Two trenches
of decay down the cheeks,
        the dress wearing itself
away, the heart's embroidered
        harness. And inside
never intended to be seen,
        naked, breathing,
wormholes, striations of the grain.
        What holds the parts in place:
glue of knackered hooves.
        Such havoc the pierced hands
wrestle—the soft blue mantle of Heaven
        melts about the body,
the body shriven, its gilt
        stars of scabbed paint
flaking off. Leaven.
        How our undressings lift us . . .
A sacred thing undone grows brave,
        a convict with nothing
in the world to lose—
        the baby sheds his baby fat,
his gold hair calms, mouse-brown.
        Epiphanies glance off him then,
a human thing, and hungry.

2

Housefire

The spark struck in secret under the stairs in dust
in the cellar smolders the way a face does, and the life
inside it, after a slap. A mortification, stains

on the floor of a caged thing's cage. In dust
in the cellar where our bicycles lean
broken-antlered in the dark. Among molds

in the cellar where the cat swollen with poison
curls in the damp to extinguish herself. It's dark outside;
inside the dark becomes particles a little like rain

stilled. Behind chicken-wired glass the garden
shakes a few leaves down. Most of winter's work is done,
the pond lidded, the ruts of the bicycles' wheels

cast in iron. The fire begins by itself, a breathing-life-into,
a kindling: cells of our skin, soil from the garden;
tinder for the fire's insistence. The fire has been impatient

to begin all along. The house is its accomplice.
Roots of the black walnut hold tight the foundations,
hence nothing grows here, nothing flourishes.

But flames brush the root hairs, make them stand on end.
Like a story's ending, not quite to wake us is the fire's
intention. To stroke us with its smoke, our sleeping faces.

We Lie Like Four Spoons in a Drawer

First and fourth-born making borders
of their greatest and least bodies—
where bed touches wall,
where bed ends.

Second and third filling the center,
interior machinery:

assembly-line,
self-appointed galley of slaves.
The signal's given

to brush the barely touching
fingers along the turned back's length.

As sheets wick
what spills on them,

each sister siphons a radiant
rivalry from her successor's skin.
Never ask for whom you work . . .
Even the last on the ladder understands
how her turn comes.

First the rung above must fully burn,
and the soles of the one
ascending.

Feudal: Thus eros
arranges us.

Pear Tree

Under her breath, our mother sings
Die Lotosblume . . . Utterly tender, forever fresh,
the wound she hides will open up in us.
Its entrance a kind of spinning door, it ushers in
men no surer than shadows, then out, out,
their spectral children.
We don't will ourselves to birth. *The white light*
drew me on, a voice says from the screen. Snow falls,
obliterating blossom and the egg-yolk yellow
daffodils of a precipitous spring. Another season,
another child's conception. Quixotic,
tall, perfumed, the pear tree rises
from entanglements of backyard junk—
a Pearly Queen, a thunderhead. Everything survives
the story of its fall. Smashed statues
trash the bottom of the garden where we go secretly,
my sisters and I, to shit among nettles. In the wreckage
of the pear tree's arms an icebox lies, lead-white
under dirt. I place it there, I drag it slowly from there
to the lake. My sisters rest inside, chrysalides, recuperating
in the sleep of change. The lotus shrinks. She weakens
against the moon's older-and-wiser talk, she opens.
I was a cold child, and now my nipples stiffen,
nothing I can do to stop them, at the least chill, the truth's
(snow falling through all this uncertain time,
drifts, a shifting *then*) revision. The pear tree grows
white-hot under heaps of blossom.

As the Crow Flies, So Will It Fall

Come sunup, say, or sundown, and a neighbor's brutish dog
goes carrying it off to worry it all day, as if it were its own
foot, broken. And the cat who tastes her kittens' salt-glazed

pelts, the watery blood-flora on the bottom of the box,
she eats the afterbirth—her goblin-damson—she stains
the cold spires of her teeth. But keeps her white coat

clean. So ninny, wandering, deluded, mooncalf Cora,
"White Lady of Finchley," can call her "daughter,"
can sing to her through dusk, *My little girl* . . . In colorless

dresses, stockings, gloves, in geisha makeup,
Cora frames herself archangel. But archangels aren't female.
But fictional. But oblivious to this. Poor simple mind,

poor solid body. Her shopping basket bulges: eggs, eggs,
coupons, gizzards for her girl. But I've dreamed
of transubstantiation also. I keep my armory intact—

as you keep your brain at its scatterpearl tasks,
your body on its tensed string. But then your blood escapes,
you've *let it go,* you've *ruined your good white things,*

and strong brine might lighten the stain, but leaves
its residue, a rosy watermark. To float like fat in the soup
on every white field in the drawer, rogue nighttime

among the daylight things. Oh, Cora knows. The heart creates
its quarry: origamis, folds in frogs and cranes and crows
the flatness facing it. It aims its arrows,

cuts an eyehole, a stone's throw in the huge opaque.
You shape your kill. And what you've known comes down.
Falls far. Falls far from you. Wherever it will.

At the Edge of the Garden, a Tattooed Spider

The rosebush blooms extravagantly
all around her: *Her* roses,
her lightwires. The sun almost works

the wires, but sun's and rain's collision
at the equinox fires this: the spider's sense
is she's alone, a woman in a window

up-tipping slowly her thimbleful of sound,
her held note: C on the cliff's edge
of the tempered scale. Now rain begins

to strum the web and make inflected
music-of-breaking-things, a song the sun
burns up. But there isn't the expected

rainbow, there's a stranger time
trapped in the trees. Beginning-evening
and departing-day peel away—

will this resolve full viable,
this hour between? The woman holds
her note, the web shudders, the spider waits:

not air, not rain on her ladder's rungs.
An always-climbing caller,
always calling something far-off closer.

Phrenological

After a portrait of John Donne by Isaac Oliver

When I look at your strict triangular beard sharp as a dandy's hand-kerchief, I see the crotch of your mistress splayed in the crotch of a tree, a dwarf tree on the mound of a gibbet hill. I see you take from this nest the very tender fledglings in your mouth and carry them un-harmed to where the ill-conceived will rightly lie unblamable beside the speechless: that potter's field wherein the apple holds the worm like a safe thought carved in kindling, the worm a lighted candle. I guide my skewed-with-longing optical instrument across the topog-raphy of your outer-visible mind. By its flickering attempt interpreta-tion of your position in time. Your past-indicative skull half hidden by the glowworm skin, your smile like a litany in pig Latin. Your ter-atomatous crotch decants its few stray trickles of darkness, thrust a little to the side as a hip to bear the weight of heirs. Inverse shield, crib of shadow, cooled congealed torrent of sugar from inside a browning apple. Windfalls pitch themselves against the rigorous economies of orchards, the volatility of bodily demand, her hairs, sex-strewn, in your escutcheon beard.

Estate

The mother's mother's mother's silver: in the silver-cloth unfurled. On the dog-stained carpet, lights glinting, the gray of ashes on the worn weave. Has there been a burial at sea? Someone's sobbing—sometimes quietly and sometimes like the clash of steel. Expressions gleam in the solid silver bowls of spoons, the coin-silver, silver plate, the English, the Mexican silver spoons. Our yolk-sack faces, anamorphosed in the bowls of spoons. Sometimes impeachable decisions stop. Four odd spoons surface, the sisters let fate stir: the neck of the bottle, the straw's length, the baby's whim marries spoon to hand. Or three handles stand out and everything topples, or four too gorgeous spoons come forth and we spin the barrel of a pistol. Then riddle-spoons arise, entrails of auguries. A one-horned spoon for weighing testicles, its complement the spoon for gravid wombs, the spoon with the barbed flame for pricking sour things, with a serrated grin, the punctured spoon, the mended hybrid spoon, the spoon for the mouth of the half-human, half-animal guest at the table. The spoon with the repoussé woman clothed with the sun and the big lamp of the moon underfoot. Such riches to divide among us, such designs, such tarnish.

Childhood's House

Dogs guard each approach:
one to the widow's walk's every vantage point.
One humor for every aspect
of the wind: ill-tempered, selfless, obedient, obstinate.
Then the four daughters of the house
start to stir, then wander, then the dogs begin
slackening to fattened hogs.
And lie there sighing and melting
in the rich ground under our apple trees.
I'm the daughter who hits the dogs with sticks
for asking for too much too often.
But my hunger equals theirs: recidivist
scroungers, with what license should I shame them?
They have such finite lives. Sevens and sevens . . .
One of them as I speak, all humility, feeds a lilac bush her flesh.
Flowers of May. My birthday flowers.
My voice is a short leash. It hurts her to listen,
since she can't answer. But the others, when I don't call them in
they wander. Out of the pen of slavish
adoration into wilderness.

The Parties

We lean against, then kiss
the gargoyles: At certain gates, the nerves of the expressive tongue
fail. And the tongue that is only receptive takes over.
Cherry cake, fondant, Parma violet . . .

After, we run—our good host shooing us
over the hills and valleys of his garden,
through the malt-brown door, into the hallway's ever-wet, intestinal
treacle-brown. Then up the stairs,
then into swamps of sequins and chiffon—we choose our gowns
and change for him.

And grow pliant while he hoists us,
his meat-hook hands under our armpits, onto the wide bed,
fits us with boxing gloves bound tight
around our fists.

And let him bite off, one by one,
the buttons, and with his teeth test the skin-pearls plump between
buttonholes. Then in the mirrored room (in every drawer
a chocolate or coin jar), we watch him watch us
pummel one another tender.

He always sleeps best afterwards, he says.
Then when he leaves us reinhabiting our own plain frocks,
before we're fetched, we always fill our mouths
before our pockets.

Jack's Lake

For Joanne and Jenny

The surface of the pond we leaned across
shone like a bottle pulled from a fire,
burled with oil-swirls, buckled.
But things were moving through its rooms,
under the inverse chandeliers looped
from its mirrored ceiling. We leaned, reaching
for a paper boat becalmed past touching.
Our shadows stretched over the embezzled harbor
where our boat docked. In our hands, willow sticks,
and on the bank behind us, early fireflies
or lingering dragonflies clung to the tips
of the grasses. The sticks drew arcs in the air,
weighted like a metronome when you've
set it at the upper notch, where it nearly stops.
From afar the shape changed, turning
from animal to rusted thing to thing of wicker
or wood. Until the current drew it nearer
and we stopped wanting our lost boat,
it came unmoored from us. And we took
the stranger's endless strangeness in,
the twine around him, the annexed stone.

Anaglypta

After *The Vessels of the Female,* from Leonardo da Vinci's anatomical folios

By snakes, by ladders, you, I, to the rope,
by slow-languorous tonguing, our belt buckles unfastening,
to the scaffolds built about us (to stay, to stave off overspillings),
we clamber up elaborate, raised friezes
of our joined-at-the-umbilicus borders
(brambles and wingspans lift and intermingle,
claws, stamens, fronds, the loosed, the caged,
a lolling and lascivious tangle
predilection builds, traveling versus gravity,
trailing the scalpel, trailing the eye,
veil after veil torn a little, being drawn aside—),

clamber and descend in the moist and shaded wilderness
what rungs we stumble on—rib-and-spine espalier,
fruit trees dotted with oval fruit and round fruit
inside the body's summer orchards,
and hung in the upper branches: a mortuary moon
by which to plunder, unselectively,
anonymous body parts bought from the jailer.
Bought for a bottle of something volatile, drained, deveined,
pried open by the anatomist—moved, raised, levered open,
the flesh and its star chamber of desires . . .
The point of entry is a locked box in a drawer,
a locket lying in the box.
The drawer is a trick drawer in a wall of trompe l'oeil drawers.
Inside the polished locket, reflected back, the anxious stare . . .

Climbing the hieratic thorns, our secret jealousies.
Climbing the brambles where the cat is snagged who caught the
    songbird instantly the dark came down.

Cock Robin

Not eat the thing you took. Not pluck its feathers, peel its skin.
Not kiss your own face on the mouth, imagining
the tasting. Nor bury the thing you bring down from the sky.

Not interpret the meaning of its cry. Not clothe the cooling thing
in woolens. Not reel it in. Not wind it while it writhes.
Not breathe hard while you work, not speak of it, not burrow in.

But barely look upon the garden where the weight fell, sudden.
Where the falling broke it open, the plummet stopped.
Where rain falls down in dying angles and damage blooms.

Not touch the entry wound. Not stitch it up. Nor enter.
Not with a finger. Not the Viking eye. Not wonder.
But leave be what you took. But let what spills congeal.

And wager everything you own the grass grows over it in time.
It cannot rise again. The sky assists this with its rain.
And the garden, and the mind.

At Ravenscroft

Above, it's still raining, pins falling,
microscopic bells tolling among the needles.
The hill juts out a little from the cemetery,
sheltered by cedars of Lebanon,
neutral ground, not for the dead but their visitors.
If you opened the hill, you'd find no evidence inside of death,
only hovering above the opening
a folly, a bench of ivied, blackened iron,
a drinking fountain kept operative for the living.
We've climbed the hill together, we're tired and thirsty
but don't want to drink from the fountain.
We shake out and let down our umbrellas in raggedy unison—
so little rain filters through the canopy—
but the air's sodden and drops of water bead our faces.
Aspects of all of us glisten in them,
too negligible for the unassisted eye.
You might think we'd stopped to count ourselves,
or for a photograph, we stand so well composed,
growing smaller and smaller.
We stand near the fountain where "Tranquility"
in gothic script on a green-rimed copper plate fairly shines.
Behind the fountain, the vista has no borders.
Intact and broken stones, pell-mell, melt affectionately
into a vanishing point just below the horizon.
One sister bends over "Tranquility," while the next waits her turn.
Each puts her mouth to it, it seems a long, long time.

3

Bright Ardor

The house beneath its sheath of roiled light
shimmers, a kind of bride. Almond trees
in front brocade the sky, air veils the doors
and windows: The lot runs
out from under us, a rained-on painting,
river of space. Under the film
of heat the facade is a kind of cover,
coaxing and dissembling. It draws us in
and closes, and the contents run amok:
Ladders melt, stair rails cling red hot
and twisted to a wall. The rooms we want to enter
disappear, the way to them a turning vine,
impossible to climb, but flowering up and down,
blistering. Identities shift—families
of foxes under the beds, wolves in the attic,
a cat's cries turning human: *Feed me,*
fill me with reprieve. A lifelike baby-doll
mimics a baby left behind, and the fireman falls
for her, he gives the life she asks for, fixed
imploring arms extended from the crib. Small hands
strike matches. Fevers fly out, furies
fly out from the place of gestation, of origin.
Like the white silk-satin of *Taste not of the tree,*
which is a furled bud in the wood that framed the house,
a locked thing longing for a key.

L'Atlante

Does the shining of the passing fields signal
as the silence does
a glimpse into a life's lining
(like a cloak's)
which, like a leaf fallen,
travels the canals?

Her reflection yawns, shallow pool
she will stand at the bank of to drink.

The banks are veiled
in water lifted from the world
and dropped again.
How the waterlight of one suspended dream
drowns everything:

mother's hair
escaping its silk scarf in the wind;
gesture of the father's hand
on his uncertain hat, blood ties.

Image she is.
Image she shall marry.
Wary of its edge,

she'll travel
several times toward the pool
forming and reforming in her path
to fool her. We'll watch her
drown herself forgetting

intention is a web
without the tensile strength to hold us.

The Betrothal

Bees, or birds bickering
in all directions,

I come slowly
to my senses,
a process begging
capture.

Mourning doves
drive and drive their dull
apologies home.
The fog reroutes them.

I'm not tempted to follow.
Flesh on flesh deliquesces,
lies lapsed, lies leaking,
pupal—

an elaboration of limbs:
the way two cherries make an earring
dangle, a glistening
participle—

at each fork,
plenitude suspended
near the pulse of
something to be appended to.

Birthmark

In my ninth month I ached for the savor of blackcurrants: a fruit of elsewhere, out of season. And since his birth he's carried a map of that place on his instep. A place more private than the sex of a boy, which he can never quite hide. I thought my craving signified the daughter whose dresses I store. Which, when I have a second boy, I'll bury. A summer frock writhes on the line in the wind, a white and blue grid with one small-as-aphid *i* inside each square—as in a glass specimen box, a room you can look into from all sides. My "Book of God-fear" warns of *good women who love to account for every defect in their children by the doctrine of longing* . . . but my boy's sex is no defect. And the mark on his foot is only my burden if my fault, only my fault if you can blame me. There was a mother whose huge desire for oysters she couldn't satisfy. And when her child came with rough scurf on his hands and feet that mimicked the shells of those so-wanted morsels, something foreign fled from her, slipped into the night and locked the door behind it. Should she go after it? Well my daughter knows to run from me, to leave her clothing empty. I'd gorge on any rare commodity to bring her forth. I'll travel to the shore and trawl until the sea-muck makes a mountain on the sand and gives to this bad hunger a body.

Passerine

Questioning again, or singing
     or signaling, at the crossing
          of borders in air, the fixed

horizon dissolving.
     Certain, then shifting.
          After a winter, spring

rain and rash breezes
     install in her such trembling,
          as if a bough might break

beneath her—a smaller war
     within a ceasefire,
          this work, this balancing:

Between gravity and levity,
     my listening wanders
          again,

I hear: *If air I am,*
     how am I anchored,
          if earth, why have I wings?

Room, window, shining surface
     of uncertain center . . .
          Field, motion, wave of wind:

lake yielding to warmer air,
     slip of water risen,
          one crop of clouds

lusher than all the others—forgotten south . . .
     Already leaving this
          garden far behind,

a constancy of wordless sound,
    the air divides the leaves.
        Deep in their shining the lyric splits,

debuts the shy twin,
    sister music—a scale
        too intricate for the ear.

Boy Pouring Water

Bitten about the face and neck,
bitten and burned, but not coming to my call.
Would you sit a hundred years
on your haunches in the grass, stone still?
Don't the enchanted turn to stone?
Slingshot boys, birds in mid-flight,
dogs cocking their legs, the baker's fat,
floured hands on his table.
Until the crusts on the loaves mold over.
Who wouldn't give up flesh and blood for something less
liable? Your ears throb—someone talks about you
every minute, and every tooth shoves
a blunt blade through you.
But hurts are your richest assets:
cuts for coin, kisses and breasts brimming milk
for merchandise. Your cheeks shine,
angry, wet, red. As if they're lit.
As if you kept St. Lucy's crown of candles
hid inside. And the mayflies swarm
round your sweet salted skin,
the fruit of your cheeks like lanterns.
I think these flies will hum all century.
But you won't listen, won't swivel on your heels
when I call your name. On your haunches
in the grass, spooning water from one bowl to another,
pouring water from cup to metal can.
But the weather will turn, the nonstop turning
of the seasons turn you to nothing.

Bestial

A child will stray, will strain against the leashes
of the stories. But the apple basket beckons,
the reddest apple oozes poison.
And the girl must choose it. The girl must grow
devoted to the lovely. And this is hers: beauty's double
blade. One edge grinds the other, the good child
sharpens and grows real. Only beauty is a restless bleed.
It rises to the skin, a deep contusion, spills
its port-wine stain from face to face. And clouds roll,
and the boy just now entering goes following his ball.
His leash is endless, his plot more mist than land,
and space around him turns, seems to hold,
but wavers at the border, changes. Undevoted air . . .
Only a vacant chair where his mother sat—minutes
or hours ago. Clink of ice in her glass gone, the safety net
of watching taken. Only a different garden.
Two swings rusting in their frame, a spider's rose-window
glimmer in the roses, one genie's shoe
of silver leather on the path. Dropped abruptly, again
picked up and dropped, the child's Russian doll
of play-within-play. Shining shield and breastplate,
sword and scabbard, dropped. Parasols. A garden hose half coiled—
not a serpent's dark and darker coils, but grass-green plastic:
object-duplicity the lost boy shrinks from
as pink clouds above him contract in the robin's egg sky—
a sweetness cringing at the edges.
He stands there like a glass of water on the grass,
a clear form of distortion, and aloneness drains him.
Where has his mother gone? The boy's face
is fragile, almost transparent pale, foxed with sun-gold
splashes. And the lashes: The blue eyes suffer
a surfeit of them, tiny scythes, black, baroquely curved.
He's too beautiful by far. The boy must not be so.
The girl must harm him, the girl must shake this

false north, this magnetic center. The boy's frailty,
his pale thin limbs and shining hair transgress,
his golden gesture of lostness, his red mouth glistening—
red, alizarin crimson—and wet, like a rose
in a book. Story of Beauty. *Knees knocking each other,*
with a look so piteous, as if to tell . . .
To start with, she must touch him, and touching, find him
real. A real child, not immortal, imagined, ideal—
white as snow, black as ebony, blood-drop fallen on the snowy sill . . .
The air is cold, though the Indian summer noon is hot
and the flowers wait unwatered. Water them in hot sun
and their scalded heads will wither, as the real child will
beneath his counterfeit perfection. Take him
by the wrist, hard, and lead him to the shade garden
at the path's end. Because the darkness is insistent there,
the chill, the soft logs filled with beetles, clockwork army tanks,
and the boy is what he must not be. Break him
a tiny bit. Look into him hard enough to wound him. A tiny bit.
  I mean:
Let the eye's stillness magnify the rigor of appraisal. He will not win.
Burn him with your look, his lovely skin.

The Lost Head

A short way across without the bindings
that should protect the feet or prevent them from wandering—
snail-trail of dragged dressing-gown cord through wet grass,
silver of stroked-backward follicles,
tentative, stilted steps, as of a body whose nerves are severed
but whose tissues begin to overgrow the leg braces—
to meet the look that has fumed up all night from the garden.
It can be a measured walk, because the look's expectancy
waits and won't retreat—
not a ball rolling from you, not a ring dropped in deep water.
But locked in place as a baby waiting to be born.
And the going-toward a slow labor
of deposition—snow morphing thorn to swan—
but with a pressured urgency, as of marrow cells
that colonize the catacombs of an implanted bone.
The white eyes in the marble head of the minor prophet or angel
or anonymous nineteenth-century industrialist—
long forgotten—watch you from the grass.
Of no importance, the departed fiction of the costume,
what the missing part of the statue might have to show for itself—
wings, or scourge marks, or pocket watch.
Without the body the head lolls in its small pool of shadow,
enormous unstrung pearl or knob of knucklebone.
And the moon overexposes everything, an x-ray, magnesium
floodlight laying bare the garden's cavities—
though the garden is black, single, unripe apples flash above you,
and the foxgloves and laburnum pods are bright as gristle.
And the jingling money plant. You step over,
without harming, the magpie splayed a few inches from the door,
its wings like fluorescent white paper fans, immaculate
paper folded and folded and torn by hand. A magic trick.
The magpies think they own the garden, though not even
in the least sense are they welcome.

The cats hunt them, snap their necks cleanly, drop them
by the door. But you cross the doorsill without stopping.
And your shadow precedes you, inverted train
of black ermine or black weightless lace.
It projects itself across the grass as if to kiss the white head,
to accost it. Your sleeping self: intention
hidden in it like a virus, murmur from a hole in the heart.
I won't decipher what it expects or wants. The neighbor boy
shining his flashlight through the tall fence won't.
He thinks the knothole is his secret. But we've seen him
steal his glimpses, seen him piss on each thing
growing in his mother's garden—like a little dog.
The boy's a sneak thief, a marauder. We all have our own
transactions to perform.
But no one will punish him. Nor us.
This is the garden of exemption. All goods priceless and unguarded.
And the cats trot across the moonlit grass.
And the magpies watch them.

Red Wing

A red-winged blackbird watches over us. All we have
to speak of at the metal table, beneath the dripping eaves,
is sleep. How many months of wakefulness

have rained on us. Since the child's cry struck the clock
on the wall, and the clock fell. A Book of Hours, the child's
expression says *sew, reap, cut wood for winter fires* . . .

We're waiting for the child to take the habit of sleep.
Waiting as the dead wait for the sennet.
The child sleeps only as he nurses, as he wishes.

But not when we wish. Never at night. He knows
to keep us wide awake to guard him. But a woman might press
a pillow down on the sleepless face, a man recall

how it was before the face and go back.
The face, the pinched face shapeless
as a waterdrop at first, then filling with reflections.

The father might forget the child. But the mother, never.
The red-wing's vigilant eye on the high beech branch.
The child sleeps, our heads hurt, the long wait

hurts, the listening for the kernel of the day to crack,
the black sky to crack and let the blue out.
All our wet shoes herded on hot air vents to dry.

No sun, no inkling of warm weather all spring.
And no sleep to soothe us. What denouement does
when it doesn't come. Before the child came, I waited,

I grew fat and thin, grew filmier of skin.
I was like the waterdrop you are when you are born—
easily shattered, easily gathered up again intact.

The Book of Labors cautions: mark the stations
of the year, the seasons. But a laborer
might put an end to such a stationless condition,

such a shapeless task, and lose no sleep.
The red-wing marches the length of the branch.
Surveyor of disquiet.

He sees a metal table, a man, a woman
cradling her head in her arms, not touching:
carillon of broken bells—sick, hung-over crier

come to call the bright world out . . .
We keep a curfew all day long. All days. And nights:
Wake up, we call, *wake up!* We want to dazzle him

with stars, but the child takes up his bow against us.
He guards his sleep. Keeps the only key.
No entry. No stars. The child won't rouse—

cloud cover evolving and devolving over us,
ink spill like the ruse of the squid, face of the deep,
expressionless. Pea soup, cauldron

of thunderheads. Then the sky leaks, little by little.
Thou that sleepest, what is sleep?
The red-wing vanishes and returns, intermittent,

and I'm surprised by the bright splash on his wings each time—
mind like a stopped bell, lost the clapper,
the long sound winding round

the bell's rim long after the bell is struck . . .
I hear it: not true song, a split note, too monotonous
to bother with. *Not now* . . . Obstinate bird,

call that won't come to roost in books of birdcalls.
Bird-renegade, keeping distance. *No time . . . No time . . .*
call that forks, dividing from itself, but promising return.

The Lacemaker

Adelaide Hamilton, St. Elizabeths Hospital, Washington

Cross a meadow *en point*
in the goblet-wet of May: a twice-million spiders
like me work there. Crush each
tenderly, and tenderly they'll explain

there's a crust to slavery that tastes like cream.
A certain bovine devotion
cleans the mind, licks the bounty out of everything.
Summer's ovum factory
oozing into noon.

A stranger bid me slip my clog off
and I did. He begged me let him lick my sole.
I thought he meant to shuck that private part
of me I've sealed.

Idolatry is kith and kin to Charity,
who cannot feed her own.
One wears a stone gown clinging wet
and fluted to the other.
I've seen them twined, whiptailed
in wheat-waves' lust.

My heart grinds shut in the heat.
It hasn't a word to say
not knotted in this mist of rag
interpreted to tatters.

Affliction Is a Marvel of Divine Technique

Fall River, Massachusetts

Audry has the voice of God.
She keeps her confidences.
And the damaged seek corollaries
for their faults. They come in
hundreds to her room, holding
their limp limbs up. Lifeless limbs.
Audry fell early. Ungrown, she fell.
So minuscule, looked back upon, her time
among quotidia. Like the scattering
of towns a train passes, grazing
the silted bend of a slowed-down river
with its small light. Bearing the broken,
the traveling, the sleepless. Elsewhere.
Slowed to a near-stop, the girl's town.
Lost. But beginning to be found
again. Just now, the town's name
forked up from a page of black print,
and I saw it and thought to travel
there. Sometimes the dead come back
to their boarded-over homes. Sometimes
the dead take over. Though often-
times the living band together
to prevent them. Audry's hair grows
and currents flow through her without outlet.
Her hands open and close, morning
to evening, but own nothing.
The girl fell early. And the fallen
can remain as they were when they fell.
Still pools, silent. Hair grows
endlessly from Audry's
empty head, dark swath, silt-dark
river. But the fish swim upstream.
The ones who fell and found themselves
taken up—but not in time. But

wounded and waiting. For those
on the bank to wade out. For those
with water to stanch the flames.
For the living to let them back in.
The way my sister waits, not evidently
cut, but rent through with wanting
intervention. The vine grows
slowly, slowly up her wall.
The foothold. But wait. But wait:
This is nothing, this waiting
without end. No lamp. Audry sees
nothing in the dark, but the wounded
come for her, her eyes half closed,
hair curved around her like a bow,
a heaven-sent weapon. Audry sets
a seal upon her heart. And the hungry
hold their limp limbs up, dead lamps, unlit,
wound with wool. The chill extremities.
To be warmed. But you can't clasp them
between your hands and rub them,
kindle them to red, red pulsing.
Beyond cold. Sometimes a shattered thing
gains value. The child cracked her skull
in an empty pool. One emptied
of water for winter but full
with dead leaves, with seed-floss. Why dive
where there is no water? But this is
not a question you would ask. Not
of the weightless Audry in her bed. Whom
God has made a silent instrument.
With silence to instruct. Useful
as directions saying *go west*
a mile, then south, to those who have
no compass in their heads. As I

have none. Turn me once and I'm lost.
Send me down a spiral staircase
and I'll not find my way home again.
Audry's heart has stopped and been
well bruised, being begun again.
Wherefore beginning
an endless thing? Her head is propped
up, read to twice a day. *Long ago,*
in a distant land . . . Once, far off,
another time . . . And music played
to it. And stopped. And the shades
behind her raised and lowered. Audry
keeps her promise. Hard as a marble
apple in a bowl. Cold in its glass
flesh. Not for swallowing.

Wedding Night

I'd climbed so far the ladder of my longing,
worked hard to glow

among the sinking and resurrecting shadows,
the jostled lanterns
under the chapel's eves. Every swan-neck and gloved hand bent

to fidget with and fine-tune my veil, as if beneath it
burned a single tenuous candleflame in a flooded cellar
or crocus broken open in dead of winter.

All night, while you kept my ruched avalanche hitched up
        almost over my head,
a black dog five hands high prowled outside.

Not a literal omen, his sleek substance—
superlative, masculine, shadowy sign without meaning—

no, though this is what I'd called for.

Pilferer, rifler, filcher.

Miranda Field was born and raised in North London. A winner of the Discovery/The Nation Award and a teaching fellow at the 2002 Bread Loaf Writers' Conference, she received her undergraduate degree from the New School and holds an MFA in poetry from Vermont College. She lives in New York City with her husband, the poet Tom Thompson, and their two children. *Swallow* is her first collection of poetry.